Mountains

Ruth Thoms

Explore the world with **Popcorn** - your complete first non-fiction library.

Look out for more titles in the Popcorn range. All books have the same format of simple text and striking images. Text is carefully matched to the pictures to help readers to identify and understand key vocabulary.
www.waylandbooks.co.uk/popcorn

Published in 2014 by Wayland

Wayland
Hachette Children's Books
338 Euston Road
London NW1 3BH

Wayland Australia
Level 17/207 Kent Street
Sydney NSW 2000

Produced for Wayland by
White-Thomson Publishing Ltd
www.wtpub.co.uk
+44 (0)843 208 7460

Editors: Steve White-Thomson/Alice Harman
Designer: Amy Sparks
Picture researcher: Ruth Thomson/Steve White-Thomson
Series consultant: Kate Ruttle
Design concept: Paul Cherrill

British Library Cataloguing in Publication Data
Thomson, Ruth, 1949-
Mountains. -- (Geography corner)(Popcorn)
1. Mountains--Juvenile literature.
I. Title II. Series
910.9'143-dc22
ISBN: 978 0 7502 8431 8

Wayland is a division of Hachette Children's Books, an Hachette UK company.
www.hachette.co.uk

First published in 2011 by Wayland

Printed and bound in China

Picture Credits: **Dreamstime**: Limp 5, Jgroup 2/10, Cristalloid 13, Krk 15, Scatto Selvaggio 17, Jianchun 18, Karl_kanal 19, Mik122 22, Leaf 22, Bsani 22; **Neil Thomson**: Neil Thomson 23; **Shutterstock**: Evgeny Murtola (cover), Vaclac Volrab 4, Scott Kapich 6, Graeme Shannon 7, Pichugin Dmitry 7, Momentum 7, Craig Hanson 1/11, Kenneth Keifer 12, Snowbelle 14, Trudy Simmons 14, vblinov 16, Image Focus 20, Robert Lascar 21, Anthony Berenyi 22, mikie11 22, Tatiana Popova 22, Gunnar Pippel 22.

Illustrations on pages 6-7, 8 and 9 by Stefan Chabluk.

Contents

What is a mountain?

A mountain is a very high hill.
Its sides are often steep and rocky.
Some mountains have a pointed top called a peak.

There are mountains under the sea, as well as on land.

This is a famous mountain in Switzerland called the Matterhorn.

The air becomes cooler and clearer as you climb a mountain. At the top, it is very cold and windy.

People always dress warmly for walking in snow, and climbing mountains.

Mountains of the world

Mountains cover more than a quarter of the Earth. Many are part of a group called a range. Some mountain ranges stretch for hundreds of miles.

Mount McKinley, Alaska

The height of a mountain is measured from sea level.

Mount Everest is the highest mountain in the world. It is covered with snow all year round, because it is too cold for the snow to melt.

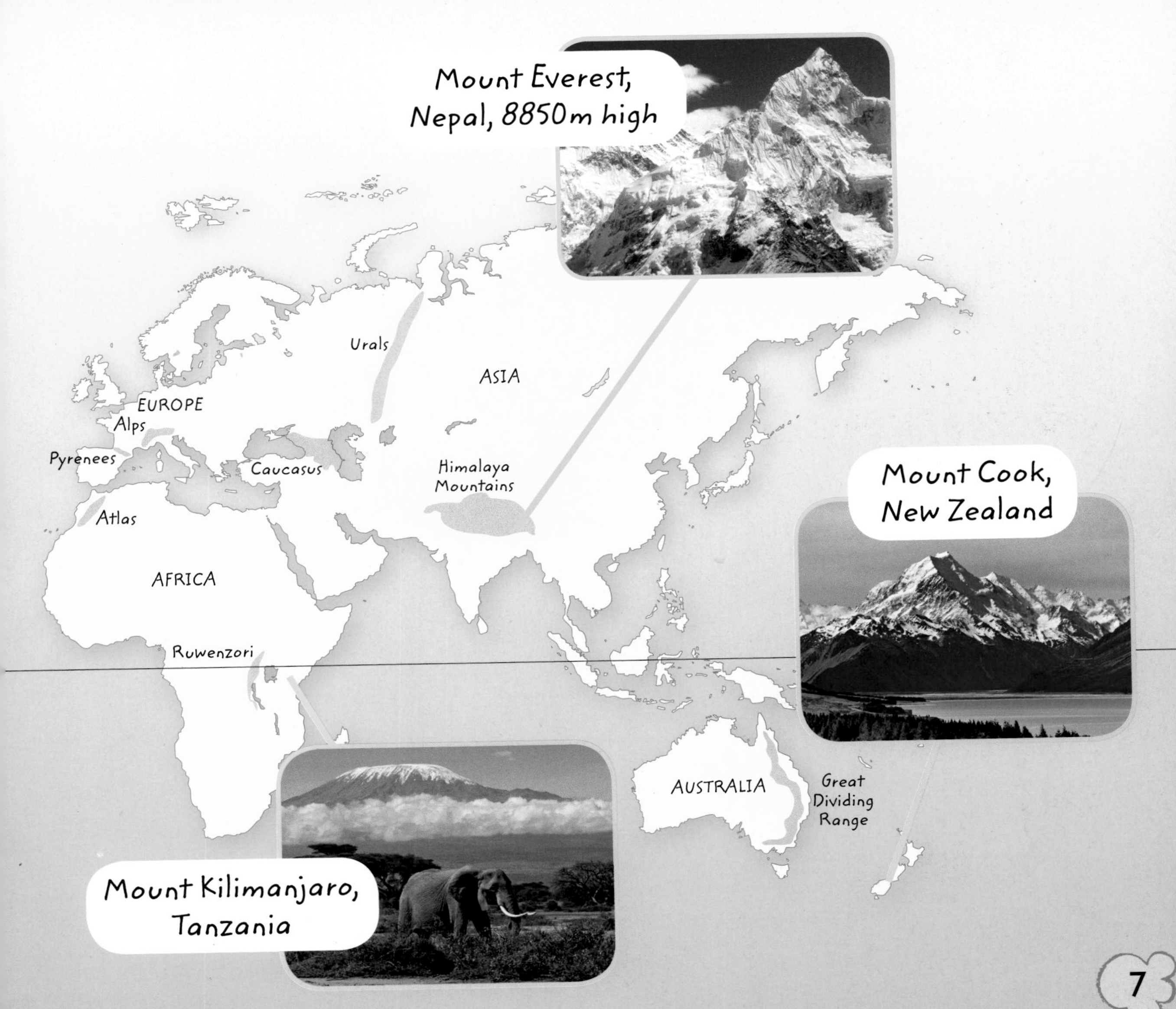

How are mountains made?

The Earth has a crust of rock. This is broken into massive pieces called plates, which have gaps between them. These move very, very slowly on top of hot liquid rock called magma.

The plates fit together like jigsaw pieces.

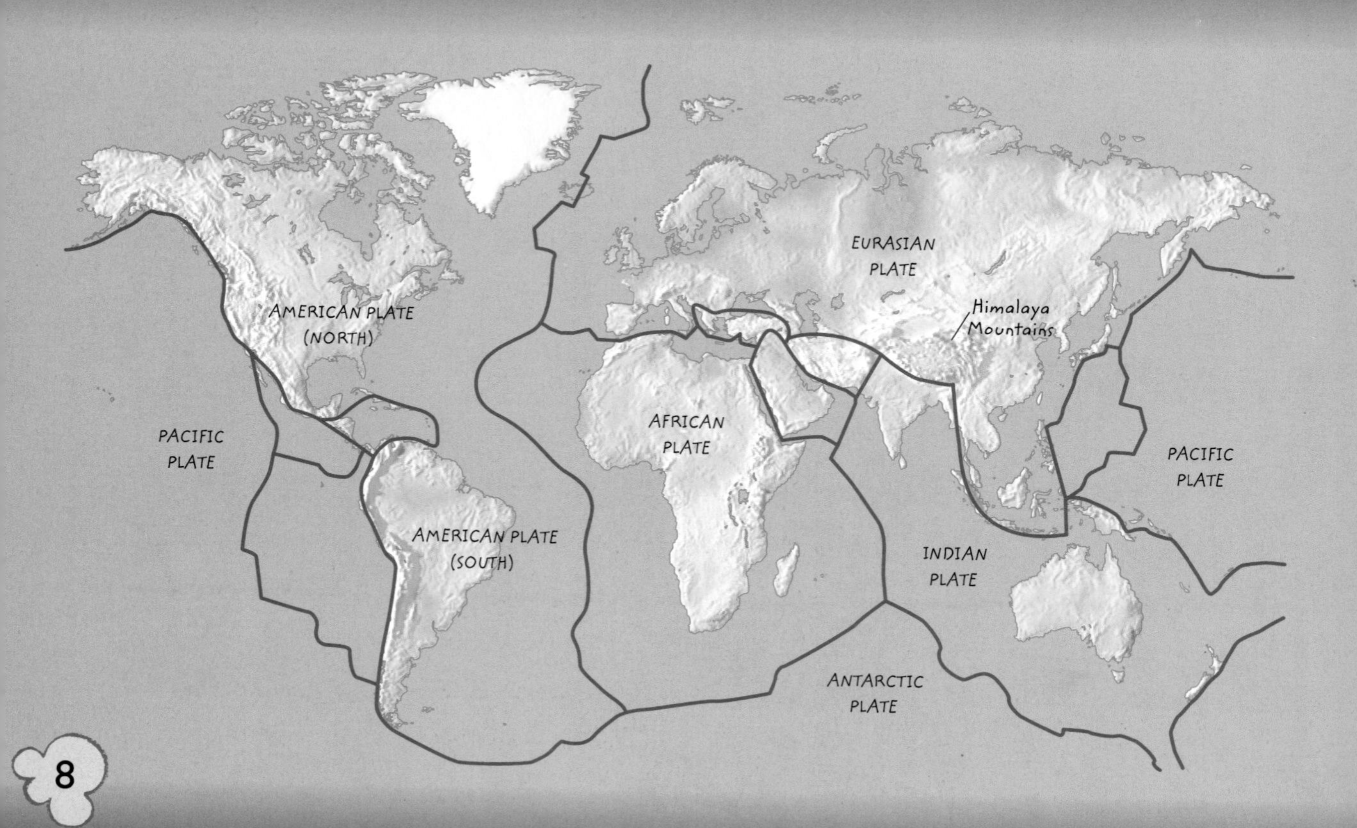

Millions of years ago, the plates crashed into each other. Some of the rocky crust was pushed upwards to form mountains.

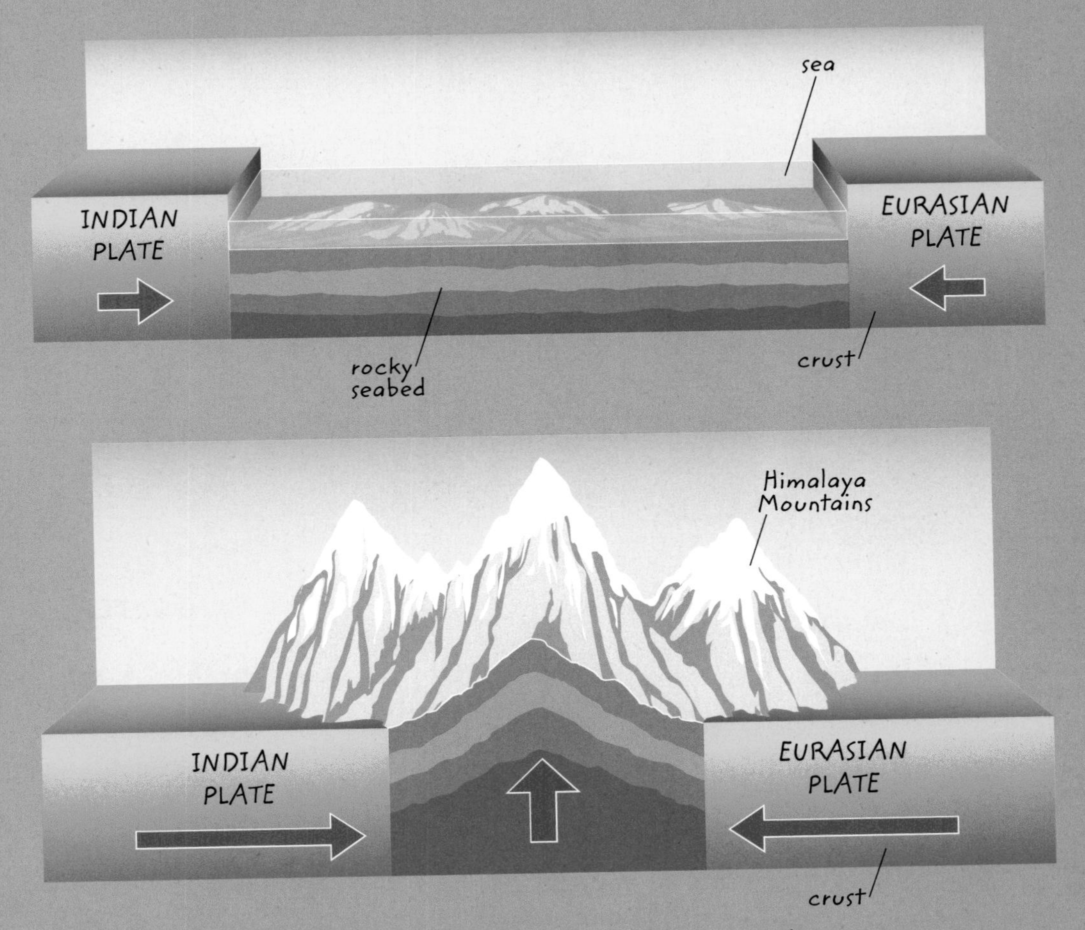

The Himalaya mountains were formed when two plates collided and pushed up the rocky seabed between them.

Volcanoes

Some mountains are formed by volcanoes. Magma from deep in the Earth erupts through a crack in the Earth's crust.

Dust and smoke, and hot rocks called lava, burst into the air when a volcano erupts.

The hole in a volcano is called its crater.

When the lava cools,
it hardens into hard rock.
Layers of rock build up to
form a cone-shaped mountain.

A volcano that no longer erupts is called an extinct volcano. Mount Fuji in Japan is an extinct volcano.

Changing shape

Water and ice slowly change the shape of mountains. Rain falls into cracks in the rocks. At night, the water freezes. The ice splits open the rocks, and pieces fall off.

The loose pieces of rock are called scree.

Rivers of ice called glaciers slide down some mountains. They move a few metres every year. The moving ice wears away the rock on the mountainsides.

A glacier created this wide valley.

Trees and flowers

Trees that need warmth and water grow on the lower slopes of mountains. Only pine trees grow on higher slopes.

Pine trees have bendy branches, so they do not break under the weight of heavy snow.

The narrow, waxy leaves of pine trees do not dry out in fierce winds.

Mountain flowers have short stems and small leaves, and grow in clumps. This helps them to survive in wind and snow.

Long roots hold mountain flowers in place.

Gentians only open when the sun shines.

Mountain animals

Mountain goats and sheep are good climbers. Goats have hooves that grip well on steep rocks.

Goats often rest on narrow ledges where hungry wolves cannot reach them.

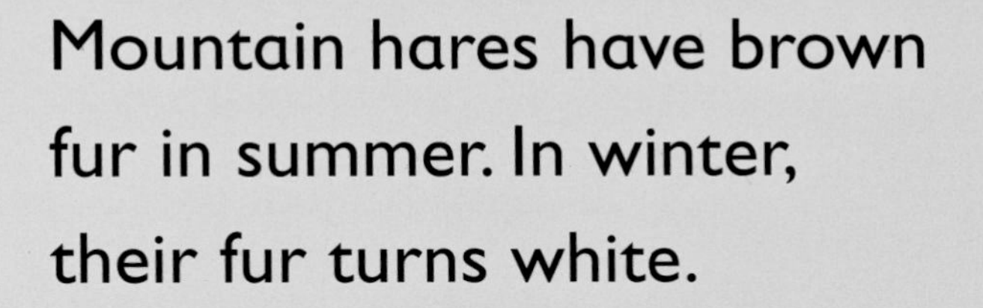

Mountain hares have brown fur in summer. In winter, their fur turns white.

The hare's white fur makes it hard to see against the snow.

Mountain farmers

Mountain slopes are too steep for growing crops. Farmers cut wide, flat steps called terraces into the lower slopes. Stony walls keep the soil and water in place.

Rice grows in pools of water on these terraces in China.

In some places, the soil is too stony for crops. Farmers keep sheep, goats, llamas or yaks instead. These animals provide milk, meat and wool.

Yaks are useful for carrying heavy loads.

Mountain transport

Roads and railway lines go through tunnels in the mountains and cross valleys on viaducts.

This Swiss train goes through 91 tunnels and crosses 291 bridges.

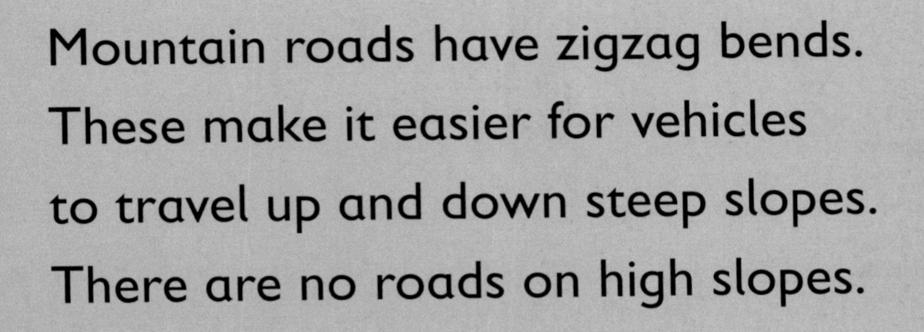

Mountain roads have zigzag bends. These make it easier for vehicles to travel up and down steep slopes. There are no roads on high slopes.

Cable cars carry skiers to the start of ski runs on mountaintops.

A mountain trip

Mountain walkers and climbers need to be ready for all kinds of weather. Why do you think they need to take each of these things with them?

watch

torch

gloves

fleece

compass

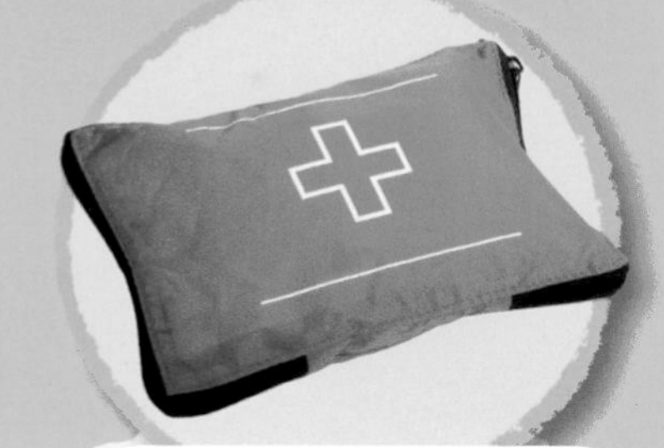

first aid kit

mobile phone

Answers:
watch for seeing how long the walk has taken
torch for seeing at night
first-aid kit in case of accidents
extra fleece and gloves in case it gets cold
compass for finding the way
mobile phone for calling in an emergency

Make a model volcano

Make a model of an erupting volcano with lava exploding out of the top.

You will need:

- a paper plate
- scissors
- paint and paintbrush
- card and glue

1. Cut the plate in half. Paint one side black.

2. Curve the plate into a cone. Overlap the edges, leaving a hole at the top. Glue them together.

3. Cut sprays of lava from coloured card. Cut a slit in each one.

4. Slot the sprays of lava onto the cone of the volcano.

Glossary

cable car a car that hangs from wires and carries people up steep slopes

clump a thick mass of plants growing close together

crust the thin, rocky outer layer of the Earth

erupt to throw out liquid rock, ash, dust and smoke

glacier a huge river of ice moving slowly down a valley

ledge a shelf of rock coming out from the side of a cliff or mountain

peak the pointed top of a mountain or hill

survive to stay alive

tunnel a long passage through rock and earth, often underground

valley a low area of land between two hills or mountains

viaduct a high bridge carrying a road or railway over a river or valley

Index